KIDNEY FRIENDLY
SMOOTHIES

Improve kidney function, Heal Your Body, and Regain
Confidence with 101 renal diet drinks recipes.

ALICE BENNISON

Disclaimer

This publication is designed to provide competent and reliable information regarding the subject matter covered. However, it is sold with the understanding that the author
is not engaged in rendering professional or nutritional advice. Laws and practices often vary from state and country to country and if medical or other expert assistance is required, the services of a professional should be sought. The author specifically disclaims any liability that is
incurred from use or application of the content of this book.

TABLE OF CONTENTS

INTRODUCTION 9

RENAL SMOOTHIES 9

"Restore The Health of Your Kidney" 9

APPLE-MANGO MADNESS SMOOTHIE 9

APPLE AND CINNAMON SMOOTHIE 11

APPLE KALE CUCUMBER SMOOTHIE 12

AVOCADO KALE SMOOTHIE 13

AVOCADO BLUEBERRY SMOOTHIE 14

AVOCADO, CELERY & PINEAPPLE SMOOTHIE 15

AVOCADO AND APPLE SMOOTHIE 16

AVOCADO-BLUEBERRY SMOOTHIE 17

BASIC FRUIT SMOOTHIE 18

BASIL STRAWBERRY MANGO SMOOTHIE 19

BLUEBERRY BANANA PROTEIN SMOOTHIE 20

BREAKFAST ALMOND MILK SHAKE 21

BFF SMOOTHIE 22

BERRY PEACH SMOOTHIE 23

CANTALOUPE BLACKBERRY SMOOTHIE 24

CANTALOUPE KALE SMOOTHIE 25

CAULIFLOWER VEGGIE SMOOTHIE 26

CHIA AND BERRIES SMOOTHIE BOWL 27

CHEF V'S SMOOTHIE BOWL 28

CHERRY AND VANILLA PROTEIN SHAKE 29

CHIA-POMEGRANATE SMOOTHIE 30

CHOCOLATE BANANA SMOOTHIE 31

CREAMY MANGO SMOOTHIE 32

CRANBERRY-PUMPKIN SMOOTHIE 33

CREAMY STRAWBERRY & CHERRY SMOOTHIE 34

CUCUMBER SMOOTHIE 35

EASY MANGO BANANA SMOOTHIE 36

EASY MANGO LASSI 37

FIG SMOOTHIE WITH CINNAMON 38

FRUIT SMOOTHIE 39

GREEN JUICE 40

GINGERBREAD & PUMPKIN SMOOTHIE 41

GLOOMY DAY SMOOTHIE 42

HAPPY SKINNY GREEN SMOOTHIE 43

HOLLY GOODNESS SMOOTHIE 44

HONEY-MANGO SMOOTHIE 45

HONG KONG MANGO DRINK 46

HEARTY PEAR AND MANGO SMOOTHIE 47

HONEY AND WILD BLUEBERRY SMOOTHIE 48

JACK-O'-LANTERN SMOOTHIE BOWL 49

KALE-PINEAPPLE SMOOTHIE 50

MANGO & ROCKET (ARUGULA) SMOOTHIE 51

MANGO-PEAR SMOOTHIE 52

MEDITERRANEAN SMOOTHIE 53

MIX BERRY CANTALOUPE SMOOTHIE 54

MOROCCAN AVOCADO SMOOTHIE 55

OATS BERRY SMOOTHIE 56

ORANGE, CARROT & KALE SMOOTHIE 57

PEANUT BUTTER CUP PROTEIN SHAKE 58

PEANUT BUTTER AND STRAWBERRY SMOOTHIE 59

PINEAPPLE & CUCUMBER SMOOTHIE 60

RASPBERRY VANILLA SMOOTHIE 61

SIRT FOOD COCKTAIL 62

SOURSOP SMOOTHIE 63

SPINACH AND BERRY SMOOTHIE 64

STRAWBERRY RHUBARB SMOOTHIE 65

SWEET CRANBERRY NECTAR 66

VEGAN BLUEBERRY SMOOTHIE 67

WALNUT & DATE SMOOTHIE 68

"Improve Kidney Fuction" 69

BLACKBERRY CHEESECAKE KETO BREAKFAST SMOOTHIE 69

CHOCOLATE PEANUT BUTTER KETO SMOOTHIE 70

CINNAMON SMOOTHIE 71

COCONUT CHERRY VANILLA SMOOTHIE 72

CUCUMBER CELERY MATCHA KETO GREEN SMOOTHIE 73

STRAWBERRY SMOOTHIE 74

STRAWBERRY VANILLA SMOOTHIE 75

EGGNOG SMOOTHIE 76

PECAN PIE SMOOTHIE 77

STRAWBERRY AVOCADO SMOOTHIE 78

"Energize Your Body" 79

AVOCADO SMOOTHIE 79

AVOCADO TURMERIC SMOOTHIE 80

BANANA & STRAWBERRY SMOOTHIE 81

BERRY MINT SMOOTHIE 82

BERRY & SPINACH SMOOTHIE 83

BLACKBERRY SMOOTHIE 84

BLUEBERRY SMOOTHIE 85

CANTALOUPE & PAPAYA SMOOTHIE 86

CINNAMON ROLL SMOOTHIE 87

COCONUT SPINACH SMOOTHIE 88

GREENIE SMOOTHIE 89

KEY LIME PIE SMOOTHIE 90

OATS COFFEE SMOOTHIE 91

ORANGE CARROT SMOOTHIE 92

PEANUT BUTTER BANANA SMOOTHIE 93

PEANUT BUTTER SMOOTHIE WITH BLUEBERRIES 94

PEACH & APRICOT SMOOTHIE 95

RASPBERRY AND PEANUT BUTTER SMOOTHIE 96

STRAWBERRY CHEESECAKE SMOOTHIE 97

STRAWBERRY, KALE AND GINGER SMOOTHIE 98

TROPICAL SMOOTHIE 99

WATERMELON & CANTALOUPE SMOOTHIE 100

"Heal Your Body and Mind" 101

AVOCADO & SPINACH SMOOTHIE 101

BERRY SMOOTHIE 102

CHOCOLATY AVOCADO SMOOTHIE 103

CUCUMBER & GREENS SMOOTHIE 104

KIWI & CUCUMBER SMOOTHIE 105

GRAPES & KALE SMOOTHIE 106

GREEN VEGGIE SMOOTHIE 107

GREEN PROTEIN DETOX SMOOTHIE..108

MANGO PINEAPPLE GREEN SMOOTHIE 109

ORANGE AND PINEAPPLE GREEN SMOOTHIE..110

CONCLUSION **111**

INTRODUCTION

The purpose of this book is to provide you with all the necessary guidelines you need to know about smoothie making. It will take you through all the step-by-step methods you can go from being an amateur to a smoothie making professional in no time.

This cookbook can diminish your danger of specific conditions, such kidney disease, coronary illness and type 2 diabetes.

The best storage container for smoothies is a glass container. You can get either of these and store your smoothies in the fridge. You can also take your jar of smoothies anywhere.

Why Smoothies?
Smoothies are enticing in many different ways. They are always loaded with fruits and vegetables. Plus, they are raw and almost always vegan which means they are super low in calories.

RENAL SMOOTHIES

"Restore the Health of Your Kidney"

APPLE-MANGO MADNESS SMOOTHIE

Preparation Time: 5 minutes
Cooking Time: 0 minutes
Servings: 2

Ingredients:
- 1 cup frozen mango cubes
- 1/2 cup fat free milk
- 1/2 cup apple juice
- 1/2 banana
- 1 packet Classic French Vanilla Flavor Carnation Breakfast Essentials Light Start

Directions:

1. In blender, put ice, Carnation Breakfast Essentials Drink, banana, apple juice, milk and mango.
2. Blend while covering till smooth.

Nutrition:

- Calories per serving: 164;
- Carbohydrates: 33g;
- Protein: 1.4g;
- Fat: 2g;
- Sugar: 0.3g;
- Sodium: 43mg;
- Fiber: 1g

APPLE AND CINNAMON SMOOTHIE

Preparation Time: 5 mins

Cooking Time: 0 mins

Servings: 2

Ingredients:

1. apples, peeled, cored, sliced
2. tablespoons pecans
3. Medjool dates, pitted
4. ½ teaspoon vanilla extract, unsweetened
5. cups almond milk, unsweetened
6. Extra: 1 ½ tablespoon ground cinnamon

Directions:

1. Place all the ingredients in the order into a food processor or blender, and then pulse for 1 to 2 minutes until smooth.
2. Distribute smoothie between two glasses and then serve.
3. Meal Prep
4. Instructions: Divide smoothie between two jars or bottles, cover with a lid and then store the containers in the refrigerator for up to 3 days.

Nutrition:

- Calories: 363 Cal
- Fat: 12 g
- Fiber: 0 g
- Carbs: 36 g
- Protein: 60 g

APPLE KALE CUCUMBER SMOOTHIE

Preparation Time: 5 minutes

Cooking Time: 5 minutes

Servings: 1

Ingredients:

- ¾ cup of water
- ½ green apple, diced
- ¾ cup kale
- ½ cucumber

Directions:

1. Toss all your ingredients into your blender, then process till smooth and creamy.
2. Serve immediately and enjoy.

Nutrition:

- Calories: 86
- Fat: 0.5g
- Carbs: 21.7g
- Protein: 1.9g

AVOCADO KALE SMOOTHIE

Preparation Time: 5 minutes

Cooking Time: 0 minutes

Servings: 3

Ingredients:

- 1 cup of water
- ½ Seville orange, peeled
- 1 avocado
- 1 cucumber, peeled
- 1 cup kale
- 1 cup of ice cubes

Directions:

1. Toss all your ingredients into your blender, then process till smooth and creamy.
2. Serve immediately and enjoy.

Nutrition:

- Calories: 160
- Fat: 13.3g
- Carbs: 11.6g
- Protein: 2.4g

AVOCADO BLUEBERRY SMOOTHIE

Preparation Time: 5 minutes

Cooking Time: 0 minutes

Servings: 1

Ingredients:

- 1 tsp chia seeds
- ½ cup unsweetened coconut milk
- 1 avocado
- ½ cup blueberries

Directions:

1. Add all the listed fixings to the blender and blend until smooth and creamy.
2. Serve immediately and enjoy.

Nutrition:

- Calories: 389
- Fat: 34.6g
- Carbs: 20.7g
- Protein: 4.8g

AVOCADO, CELERY & PINEAPPLE SMOOTHIE

Preparation Time: 5 mins

Cooking Time: 0 mins

Servings: 1

Ingredients:

- 2oz fresh pineapple, peeled and chopped stalks of celery
- 1 avocado, peeled & de-stoned
- 1 teaspoon fresh parsley
- ½ teaspoon matcha powder
- Juice of ½ lemon

Directions:

1. Place all of the ingredients into a blender and add enough water to cover them. Process until creamy and smooth.

Nutrition:

- Calories: 306
- Cal Fat: 0 g
- Fiber: 15 g
- Carbs: 49 g
- Protein: 8 g

AVOCADO AND APPLE SMOOTHIE

Preparation Time: 5 minutes

Cooking time: 0 minute

Servings: 2

Ingredients:

- 3 c. spinach
- 1 cored green apple, chopped
- 1 pitted avocado, peeled and chopped
- 3 tbsps. chia seeds
- 1 tsp. honey
- 1 frozen banana, peeled
- 2 c. coconut water

Directions:

1. Using your blender, add in all the ingredients.
2. Process well for 5 minutes to obtain a smooth consistency and serve in glasses.

Nutrition:

- 208 Calories
- 10.1g Fat
- 6g Fiber

AVOCADO-BLUEBERRY SMOOTHIE

Preparation Time: 5 minutes

Cooking time: 0 minutes

Servings: 2

Ingredients:

- ½ cup unsweetened vanilla almond milk
- ½ cup low-fat plain Greek yogurt
- 1 ripe avocado, peeled, pitted, and coarsely chopped
- 1 cup blueberries
- ¼ cup gluten-free rolled oats
- ½ teaspoon vanilla extract
- 4 ice cubes

Directions:

1. In a blender, combine the almond milk, yogurt, avocado, blueberries, oats, and vanilla and pulse until well blended.
2. Add the ice cubes and blend until thick and smooth.
3. Serve.

Nutrition:

- Calories: 273
- Total fat: 15g
- Saturated fat: 2g;
- Carbohydrates: 28g;
- Sugar: 10g;
- Fiber: 9g;
- Protein: 10g

BASIC FRUIT SMOOTHIE

Preparation Time: 10 minutes

Cooking Time: 0 minutes

Servings: 4

Ingredients:

- 1-quart strawberries, hulled
- 1 banana, broken into chunks peaches
- 1 cup orange-peach-mango juice cups ice

Directions:

1. Mix peaches, banana and strawberries in a blender until they are pureed.
2. Blend in the juice then put ice into and keep on blending until getting wanted consistency
3. Transfer into glasses and serve.

Nutrition:

- Calories per serving: 118;
- Carbohydrates: 65g;
- Protein: 1.8g;
- Fat: 2g;
- Sugar: 0.3g;
- Sodium: 72mg;
- Fiber: 0g

BASIL STRAWBERRY MANGO SMOOTHIE

Preparation Time: 5 minutes

Cooking Time: 0 minutes

Servings: 1

Ingredients:

- leaves basil
- 1 cup frozen mango pieces hulled strawberries
- 1 cup water
- 1/4 cup white sugar, or to taste cubes ice

Directions:

1. In a blender, conflate water, strawberries, mango, and basil.
2. Put in ice cubes and sugar.
3. Repeat blending the mixture till smooth.

Nutrition:

- Calories per serving: 330;
- Carbohydrates: 54g;
- Protein: 1.2g;
- Fat: 1g;
- Sugar: 0.4g;
- Sodium: 86mg;
- Fiber: 0g

BLUEBERRY BANANA PROTEIN SMOOTHIE

Preparation Time: 5 minutes

Cooking time: 5 minutes

Servings: 1

Ingredients:

- ½ cup frozen and unsweetened blueberries
- ½ banana slices up
- ¾ cup plain nonfat Greek yogurt
- ¾ cup unsweetened vanilla almond milk
- 2 cups of ice cubes

Directions:

1. Add all the ingredients into an instant pot ace blender.
2. Blend until smooth.

Nutrition:

- Calories: 230
- Protein: 19.1 grams
- Total Fat: 2.6 grams
- Carbohydrates: 32.9 grams

BREAKFAST ALMOND MILK SHAKE

Preparation Time: 4 minutes

Cooking time: 0 minute

Servings: 2

Ingredients:

- 3 cups almond milk
- 4 tbsp heavy cream
- ½ tsp vanilla extract
- 4 tbsp flax meal
- 2 tbsp protein powder
- 4 drops of liquid stevia
- Ice cubes to serve

Directions:

1. In the bowl of your food processor, add almond milk, heavy cream, flax meal, vanilla extract, collagen peptides, and stevia.
2. Blitz until uniform and smooth, for about 30 seconds.
3. Add a bit more almond milk if it's very thick.
4. Pour in a smoothie glass, add the ice cubes and sprinkle with cinnamon.

Nutrition:

- Calories 326,
- Fat: 27g;
- Net Carbs: 6g;
- Protein: 19g

BFF SMOOTHIE

Preparation Time: 10 minutes

Cooking Time: 0 minutes

Servings: 1

Ingredients:

- 1 cup frozen strawberries
- 1 cup plain Greek yogurt
- 1 cup frozen mango chunks
- 1/2 cup 1% milk
- 1 scoop vanilla whey protein powder fresh mint leaves, or more to taste

Directions:

1. Mix protein powder, milk, mango, Greek yogurt and strawberries and conflate till smooth.
2. Put in mint leaves then pulse 4-5 times till leaves are minced.

Nutrition:

- Calories per serving: 335;
- Carbohydrates: 21g;
- Protein: 3g;
- Fat: 1g;
- Sugar: 0.6g;
- Sodium: 202mg;
- Fiber: 1g

Preparation Time: 5 minutes

Cooking Time: 0 minutes

Servings: 2

Ingredients:

- 1 cup of coconut water
- 1 tbsp hemp seeds
- 1 tbsp agave
- ½ cup strawberries
- ½ cup blueberries
- ½ cup cherries
- ½ cup peaches

Directions:

1. Toss all your ingredients into your blender, then process till smooth and creamy.
2. Serve immediately and enjoy.

Nutrition:

- Calories: 117
- Fat: 2.5g
- Carbs: 22.5g
- Protein: 3.5g

CANTALOUPE BLACKBERRY SMOOTHIE

Preparation Time: 5 minutes

Cooking Time: 0 minutes

Servings: 2

Ingredients:

- 1 cup coconut milk yogurt
- ½ cup blackberries
- 2 cups fresh cantaloupe
- 1 banana

Directions:

1. Toss all your ingredients into your blender, then process till smooth.
2. Serve and enjoy.

Nutrition:

- Calories: 160
- Fat: 4.5g
- Carbs: 33.7g
- Protein: 1.8g

CANTALOUPE KALE SMOOTHIE

Preparation Time: 5 minutes

Cooking Time: 5 minutes

Servings: 2

Ingredients:

- 8 oz. water 1 orange, peeled
- 3 cups kale, chopped
- 1 banana, peeled
- 2 cups cantaloupe, chopped
- 1 zucchini, chopped

Directions:

1. Toss all your ingredients into your blender, then process till smooth and creamy.
2. Serve immediately and enjoy.

Nutrition:

- Calories: 203
- Fat: 0.5g
- Carbs: 49.2g
- Protein: 5.6g

CAULIFLOWER VEGGIE SMOOTHIE

Preparation Time: 5 minutes

Cooking Time: 0 minutes

Servings: 4

Ingredients:

- 1 zucchini, peeled and chopped
- 1 Seville orange, peeled
- 1 apple, diced
- 1 banana
- 1 cup kale
- ½ cup cauliflower

Directions:

1. Toss all your ingredients into your blender, then process till smooth and creamy.
2. Serve immediately and enjoy.

Nutrition:

- Calories: 71
- Fat: 0.3g
- Carbs: 18.3g
- Protein: 1.3g

CHIA AND BERRIES SMOOTHIE BOWL

Preparation Time: 5 minutes

Cooking Time: 0 minutes

Servings: 2

Ingredients:

- 1 and ½ cup of almond milk
- 1 cup blackberries
- ¼ cup strawberries, chopped
- 1 and ½ tablespoons chia seeds
- 1 teaspoon cinnamon powder

Directions:

1. In a blender, combine the blackberries with the strawberries and the rest of the ingredients, pulse well, divide into small bowls and serve cold.

Nutrition:

- Calories: 182
- Fat: 3.4g
- Carbs 8.4g
- Protein 3g

Preparation Time: 10 minutes

Cooking Time: 0 minutes

Servings: 1

Ingredients:

- 1/2 cup low-fat Greek yogurt
- 1/3 cup coconut water
- 1/4 cup frozen strawberries
- 1/4 cup frozen peaches
- 1/4 cup frozen mango chunks
- 1/2 banana, chopped tbsps...
- chia seeds, divided

Directions:

1. Place peaches, mango, strawberries, banana, coconut water, yogurt, and 1 tbsp. chia seeds in a blender and blend together until mixture becomes smooth.
2. Pour into a bowl and use the remaining 1 tbsp. of chia seeds as garnish.

Nutrition:

- Calories per serving: 240;
- Carbohydrates: 33.7g;
- Protein: 5g;
- Fat: 2g;
- Sugar: 0.5g;
- Sodium: 87mg;
- Fiber: 1g

CHERRY AND VANILLA PROTEIN SHAKE

Preparation Time: 5 mins

Cooking Time: 10 mins

Servings: 2

Ingredients:

- ounces cherries, destemmed
- 1 scoop vanilla protein powder
- 1 ½ cup almond milk, unsweetened

Directions:

1. Place all the ingredients in the order into a food processor or blender, and then pulse for 1 to 2 minutes until smooth
2. Distribute shake between two glasses and then serve.
3. Meal Prep Instructions: Divide shake between two jars or bottles, cover with a lid, and then store the containers in the refrigerator for up to 3 days.

Nutrition:

- Calories: 193 Cal
- Fat: 8 g
- Fiber: 11 g
- Carbs: 38 g
- Protein: 5.2 g

CHIA-POMEGRANATE SMOOTHIE

Preparation Time: 5 minutes

Cooking time: 0 minutes

Servings: 2

Ingredients:

- 1 cup pure pomegranate juice (no sugar added)
- 1 cup frozen berries
- 1 cup coarsely chopped kale
- 2 tablespoons chia seeds
- 3 Medjool dates, pitted and coarsely chopped
- Pinch ground cinnamon

Directions:

1. In a blender, combine the pomegranate juice, berries, kale, chia seeds, dates, and cinnamon and pulse until smooth.
2. Pour into glasses and serve.

Nutrition:

- Calories: 275
- Total fat: 5g
- Saturated fat: 1g;
- Carbohydrates: 59g;
- Sugar: 10g
- Fiber: 42g;
- Protein: 5g

CHOCOLATE BANANA SMOOTHIE

Preparation Time: 5 minutes

Cooking time: 0 minutes

Servings: 2

Ingredients:

- 2 bananas, peeled
- 1 cup unsweetened almond milk, or skim milk
- 1 cup crushed ice 3 tablespoons unsweetened cocoa powder
- 3 tablespoons honey

Directions:

1. In a blender, combine the bananas, almond milk, ice, cocoa powder, and honey.
2. Blend until smooth.

Nutrition:

- Calories: 219;
- Protein: 2g
- Total Carbohydrates: 57g
- Sugars: 40g
- Fiber: 6g
- Total Fat: 2g
- Saturated Fat: <1g
- Cholesterol: 0mg
- Sodium: 4mg

CREAMY MANGO SMOOTHIE

Preparation Time: 5 minutes

Cooking Time: 0 minutes

Servings: 2

Ingredients:

- 3/4 cup cold milk
- 1/4 cup vanilla yogurt
- 3/4 tsp. vanilla extract
- 1 1/2 cups chopped fresh mango ice cubes

Directions:

- Using a blender, blend ice cubes, mango, vanilla extract, yogurt, and milk until it is all creamy and smooth.

Nutrition:

- Calories per serving: 154;
- Carbohydrates: 29.8g;
- Protein: 2g;
- Fat: 1g;
- Sugar: 0.5g;
- Sodium: 98mg;
- Fiber: 1g

CRANBERRY-PUMPKIN SMOOTHIE

Preparation Time: 5 minutes

Cooking time: 0 minutes

Servings: 2

Ingredients:

- 2 cups unsweetened almond milk
- 1 cup pure pumpkin purée
- ¼ cup gluten-free rolled oats
- ¼ cup pure cranberry juice (no sugar added)
- 1 tablespoon honey
- ¼ teaspoon ground cinnamon
- Pinch ground nutmeg

Directions:

1. In a blender, combine the almond milk, pumpkin, oats, cranberry juice, honey, cinnamon, and nutmeg and blend until smooth.
2. Pour into glasses and serve immediately.

Nutrition:

- Calories: 190
- Total fat: 7g
- Saturated fat: 0g;
- Carbohydrates: 26g;
- Sugar: 12g
- Fiber: 5g;
- Protein: 4g

CREAMY STRAWBERRY & CHERRY SMOOTHIE

Preparation Time: 5 mins

Cooking Time: 0 mins

Servings: 1

Ingredients:

- 3½ oz. strawberries
- 3oz frozen pitted cherries
- 1 tablespoon plain full-fat yogurt
- 6fl oz. unsweetened soya milk

Directions:

1. Place all of the ingredients into a blender and process until smooth. Serve and enjoy.

Nutrition:

- Calories: 132 Cal
- Protein: g 183.

CUCUMBER SMOOTHIE

Preparation Time: 5 minutes

Cooking Time: 0 minutes

Servings: 2

Ingredients:

- 1 cup of ice cubes
- 20 drops liquid stevia
- 2 fresh lime, peeled and halved
- 1 tsp lime zest, grated
- 1 cucumber, chopped
- 1 avocado, pitted and peeled
- 2 cups kale
- 1 tbsp creamed coconut
- ¾ cup of coconut water

Directions:

Toss all your ingredients into your blender, then process till smooth and creamy.
Serve immediately and enjoy.

Nutrition:

- Calories: 313
- Fat: 25.1g
- Carbs: 24.7g
- Protein: 4.9g

EASY MANGO BANANA SMOOTHIE

Preparation Time: 10 minutes

Cooking Time: 0 minutes

Servings: 1

Ingredients:

- mangos - peeled, seeded, and sliced
- bananas cups
- vanilla yogurt
- cups milk

Directions:

1. In a blender, conflate milk, vanilla yogurt, banana and mangos till smooth.

Nutrition:

- Calories per serving: 133;
- Carbohydrates: 34g;
- Protein: 3g;
- Fat: 1g;
- Sugar: 2g;
- Sodium: 72mg;
- Fiber: 0g

Preparation Time: 10 minutes

Cooking Time: 0 minutes

Servings: 4

Ingredients:

- cups plain whole milk yogurt
- 1 cup milk mangoes - peeled, seeded, and chopped
- Tsps. white sugar, or to taste
- 1/8 tsp. ground cardamom

Directions:

1. In the jar of a blender, place cardamom, white sugar, mangoes, milk, and yogurt.
2. Blend for about 2 minutes or until smooth.
3. Chill in the refrigerator until cold, about 1 hour.
4. Serve with a bit sprinkling of ground cardamom.

Nutrition:

- Calories per serving: 184;
- Carbohydrates: 48g;
- Protein: 0.8g;
- Fat: 1.8g;
- Sugar 0.6g;
- Sodium: 64mg;
- Fiber: 0.5g

FIG SMOOTHIE WITH CINNAMON

Preparation time: 5 minutes
Cooking time: 0 minutes
Servings: 1

Ingredients:
- 1 large ripe fig
- 3 dessertspoons porridge oats
- 3 rounded dessertspoons Greek yoghurt
- ½ teaspoon ground cinnamon
- 200 ml orange juice 3 ice cubes

Directions:
1. Wash and dry the fig. Chop.
2. Add all ingredients to a blender.
3. Blend well. Serve.

Nutrition:
- Calories: 152
- Carbs: 32g
- Fat: 3g
- Protein: 3g

FRUIT SMOOTHIE

Preparation Time: 5 minutes

Cooking time: 0 minutes

Servings: 2

Ingredients:

- 2 cups blueberries (or any fresh or frozen fruit, cut into pieces if the fruit is large)
- 2 cups unsweetened almond milk 1 cup crushed ice
- ½ teaspoon ground ginger (or other dried ground spice such as turmeric, cinnamon, or nutmeg)

Directions:

1. In a blender, combine the blueberries, almond milk, ice, and ginger.
2. Blend until smooth.

Nutrition:

- Calories: 125;
- Protein: 2g
- Total Carbohydrates: 23g
- Sugars: 14g
- Fiber: 5g
- Total Fat: 4g;
- Fat: <1g
- Cholesterol: 0mg
- Sodium: 181mg

Preparation Time: 5 minutes

Cooking time: 0 minute

Servings: 1

Ingredients:

- 3 cups dark leafy greens
- 1 cucumber
- ¼ cup fresh Italian parsley leaves
- ¼ pineapple, cut into wedges
- ½ green apple
- ½ orange
- ½ lemon
- Pinch grated fresh ginger

Directions:

1. Using a juicer, run the greens, cucumber, parsley, pineapple, apple, orange, lemon, and ginger through it, pour into a large cup, and serve.

Nutrition:

- 200 Calories
- 14g Fats
- 27g Protein

GINGERBREAD & PUMPKIN SMOOTHIE

Preparation Time: 15 minutes

Cooking time: 50 minutes

Servings: 1

Ingredients:

- 1 cup almond milk, unsweetened
- 2 teaspoons chia seeds
- 1 banana
- ½ cup pumpkin puree, canned
- ¼ teaspoon ginger, ground
- ¼ teaspoon cinnamon, ground
- 1/8 teaspoon nutmeg, ground

Directions:

1. Start by getting out a bowl and mix your chia seeds and almond milk.
2. Allow them to soak for at least an hour, but you can soak them overnight.
3. Transfer them to a blender. Add in your remaining ingredients, and then blend until smooth.
4. Serve chilled.

Nutrition:

- 250 Calories
- 13g Fats
- 26g protein

GLOOMY DAY SMOOTHIE

Preparation Time: 10 minutes

Cooking Time: 0 minutes

Servings: 4

Ingredients:

- 1 mango - peeled, seeded, and cut into chunks
- 1 banana, peeled and chopped
- 1 cup orange juice
- 1 cup vanilla nonfat yogurt

Directions:

1. Put the banana, mango, orange juice, and yogurt in a blender and blend until the mix is smooth.
2. Fill up clear glasses, add a bendy straw for drinking and serve!

Nutrition:

- Calories per serving: 203;
- Carbohydrates: 34g;
- Protein: 1.2g;
- Fat: 2g;
- Sugar: 2g;
- Sodium: 83mg;
- Fiber: 1g

HAPPY SKINNY GREEN SMOOTHIE

Preparation Time: 10 minutes

Cooking Time: 0 minutes

Servings: 1

Ingredients:

- green tea bags
- 1 1/2 cups boiling water packets
- Wholesome Organic Stevia cups loosely packed organic baby spinach
- 1 cup fresh or frozen mango chunks
- 1/2 green apple, chopped
- 1/2 avocado, peeled and pitted
- 1/2 cup green seedless grapes
- 1/4 cup loosely packed fresh mint leaves
- 1 (1/2- by 1/4-inch) piece fresh ginger, chopped
- 1/2 lime, juiced

Directions:

1. Get boiling water and soak the tea bags in it for 3-5 minutes.
2. Remove the tea bags and allow the tea to cool.
3. Once cooled, pour it into the blender together with the rest of the ingredients and process until it is smooth.
4. Serve right away.

Nutrition:

- Calories per serving: 222;
- Carbohydrates: 59.3g;
- Protein: 8g;
- Fat: 1.6g;
- Sugar: 2g;
- Sodium: 59mg;
- Fiber: 0g

HOLLY GOODNESS SMOOTHIE

Preparation Time: 10 minutes
Cooking Time: 0 minutes
Servings: 1

Ingredients:

- 1 mango - peeled, seeded, and chopped
- 1 small banana
- 1/2 cup frozen raspberries
- 1/2 cup almond milk
- 1/2 cup hemp milk
- 1 tsp. vanilla extract
- 1 tsp. chia seeds
- 1 tsp. hemp seeds
- 1 tsp. maca powder

Directions:

1. Blend maca powder, hemp seeds, chia seeds, vanilla extract, hemp milk, almond milk, raspberries, banana, and mango using a blender until the mixture is smooth.

Nutrition:

- Calories per serving: 383;
- Carbohydrates: 76g;
- Protein: 3g;
- Fat: 1g;
- Sugar: 1.3g;
- Sodium: 63mg;
- Fiber: 0g

HONEY-MANGO SMOOTHIE

Preparation Time: 10 minutes

Cooking Time: 0 minutes

Servings: 2

Ingredients:

- 1 mango - peeled, seeded, and cubed
- 1 tbsp. white sugar tbsps...
- Honey
- 1 cup nonfat milk
- 1 tsp. lemon juice
- 1 cup ice cubes

Directions:

1. In a blender pitcher, put sugar, honey and mango; add lemon juice and milk, conflate till smooth.
2. Distribute ice cubes among 2 serving glasses.
3. Put mango smoothie on ice, serve.

Nutrition:

- Calories per serving: 346;
- Carbohydrates: 45g;
- Protein: 1.8g;
- Fat: 2g;
- Sugar: 0.5g;
- Sodium: 58mg;
- Fiber: 0.4g

HONG KONG MANGO DRINK

Preparation Time: 10 minutes

Cooking Time: 0 minutes

Servings: 2

Ingredients:

- 1/2 cup small pearl tapioca
- 1 mango - peeled, seeded and diced ice cubes
- 1/2 cup coconut milk

Directions:

1. Over high heat, boil water.
2. When the water is boiling, mix in the tapioca pearls then boil again.
3. Uncover while cooking the tapioca pearls for 10 minutes, mixing from time to time.
4. Put the cover back then take off heat, let it rest for half an hour.
5. In a colander placed in the sink, drain well; cover then chill.
6. In a blender, blend ice and mango till smooth.
7. In 2 tall glasses, distribute chilled tapioca pearls; pour the mango mixture on top then pour on top of each with a quarter cup coconut milk.

Nutrition:

- Calories per serving: 234;
- Carbohydrates: 56g;
- Protein: 4.8g;
- Fat: 1g;
- Sugar: 3g;
- Sodium: 64mg;
- Fiber: 0g

HEARTY PEAR AND MANGO SMOOTHIE

Preparation Time: 10 minutes

Cooking time: 0 minute

Servings: 1

Ingredients:

- 1 ripe mango, cored and chopped
- ½ mango, peeled, pitted, and chopped
- 1 cup kale, chopped
- ½ cup plain Greek yogurt
- 2 ice cubes

Directions:

1. Add pear, mango, yogurt, kale, and mango to a blender and puree.
2. Add ice and blend until you have a smooth texture.
3. Serve and enjoy!

Nutrition: (Per Serving)

- Calories: 293
- Fat: 8g
- Carbohydrates: 53g
- Protein: 8g

HONEY AND WILD BLUEBERRY SMOOTHIE

Preparation Time: 5 minutes

Cooking time: 10 minutes

Servings: 2

Ingredients:

- 1 whole banana
- 1 cup of mango chunks
- ½ cup wild blueberries
- ½ plain, nonfat Greek yogurt
- ½ cup milk (for blending)
- 1 tablespoon raw honey
- ½ cup of kale

Directions:

1. Add all the above ingredients into an instant pot Ace blender.
2. Add extra ice cubes if needed.
3. Process until smooth.

Nutrition:

- Calories: 223
- Protein: 9.4 grams
- Total Fat: 1.4 grams
- Carbohydrates: 46.8 grams

JACK-O'-LANTERN SMOOTHIE BOWL

Preparation Time: 10 minutes

Cooking Time: 0 minutes

Servings: 1

Ingredients:

- 1 cup frozen mango chunks
- ¾ cup reduced-fat plain Greek yogurt
- ¼ cup reduced-fat milk
- 1 tsp. vanilla extract
- 1 strawberry, hulled and halved
- 1 tsp. chia seeds

Directions:

1. In a blender, combine vanilla, milk, yogurt, and mango.
2. Puree the mixture until smooth.
3. Pour the entire smoothie into a bowl and decorate to make the drink look like a jack-o'-lantern.
4. Use halved strawberries to make the cheeks and use the chia seeds to make eyes and a nose.
5. Serve the smoothie with a green spoon attached with a paper leaf to make it look like a pumpkin stem.

Nutrition:

- Calories per serving: 498;
- Carbohydrates: 56g;
- Protein: 1g;
- Fat: 1g;
- Sugar: 3g;
- Sodium: 36mg;
- Fiber: 1g

KALE-PINEAPPLE SMOOTHIE

Preparation Time: 5 minutes

Cooking time: 5 minutes

Servings: 2

Ingredients:

- 1 Persian cucumber fresh mint
- 1 cup of coconut milk
- 1 tablespoon honey
- 1 ½ cups of pineapple pieces
- ¼ pound baby kale

Directions:

1. Cut the ends off of the cucumbers and then cut the whole cucumber into small cubes.
2. Strip the mint leaves from the stems.
3. Add all the ingredients to your instant pot
4. Ace blender and blend until smooth.

Nutrition:

- Calories: 140
- Protein: 4 grams
- Total Fat: 2.5 grams
- Carbohydrates: 30 grams

MANGO & ROCKET (ARUGULA) SMOOTHIE

Preparation Time: 5 mins
Cooking Time: 0 mins
Servings: 1

Ingredients:

- 1oz fresh rocket (arugula)
- 5oz fresh mango, peeled, de-stoned and chopped
- 1 avocado, de-stoned and peeled
- ½ teaspoon matcha powder
- Juice of 1 lime

Directions:

1. Place all of the ingredients into a blender with enough water to cover them and process until smooth.
2. Add a few ice cubes and enjoy.

Nutrition:

- Calories: 369
- Cal Fat: 0 g
- Fiber: g
- Carbs: g
- Protein: g

MANGO-PEAR SMOOTHIE

Preparation Time: 10 minutes

Cooking time: 0 minutes

Servings: 1

Ingredients:

- 1 ripe pear, cored and chopped
- ½ mango, peeled, pitted, and chopped
- 1 cup chopped kale
- ½ cup plain Greek yogurt
- 2 ice cubes

Directions:

1. In a blender, purée the pear, mango, kale, and yogurt.
2. Add the ice and blend until thick and smooth.
3. Pour the smoothie into a glass and serve cold.

Nutrition:

- Calories: 293
- Total Fat: 8g
- Saturated Fat: 5g;
- Carbohydrates: 53g
- Fiber: 7g;
- Protein: 8g

MEDITERRANEAN SMOOTHIE

Preparation Time: 5 minutes

Cooking time: 5 minutes

Servings: 2

Ingredients:

- 2 cups of baby spinach
- 1 teaspoon fresh ginger root
- 1 frozen banana, pre-sliced
- 1 small mango
- ½ cup beet juice
- ½ cup of skim milk
- 4-6 ice cubes

Directions:

1. Take all ingredients and place them in your instant pot
2. Ace blender.

Nutrition:

- Calories: 168
- Protein: 4 grams
- Total Fat: 1 gram
- Carbohydrates: 39 grams

MIX BERRY CANTALOUPE SMOOTHIE

Preparation Time: 5 minutes
Cooking Time: 0 minutes
Servings: 2

Ingredients:

- 1 cup alkaline water
- 2 fresh Seville orange juices
- ¼ cup fresh mint leaves
- 1 ½ cups mixed berries
- 2 cups cantaloupe

Directions:

1. Toss all your ingredients into your blender, then process till smooth.
2. Serve immediately and enjoy.

Nutrition:

- Calories: 122
- Fat: 1g
- Carbs: 26.1g
- Protein: 2.4g

MOROCCAN AVOCADO SMOOTHIE

Preparation Time: 5 minutes

Cooking time: 0 minutes

Servings: 4

Ingredients:

- 1 ripe avocado, peeled and pitted
- 1 overripe banana
- 1 cup almond milk, unsweetened
- 1 cup of ice

Directions:

1. Place the avocado, banana, milk, and ice into your instant pot Ace blender.
2. Blend until smooth with no pieces of avocado remaining.

Nutrition:

- Calories: 100
- Protein: 1 gram
- Total Fat: 6 grams
- Carbohydrates: 11 grams

OATS BERRY SMOOTHIE

Preparation Time: 5 minutes
Cooking time: 5 minutes
Servings: 2

Ingredients:

- 1 cup of frozen berries
- 1 cup Greek yogurt
- ¼ cup of milk
- ¼ cup of oats
- 2 teaspoon honey

Directions:

1. Place all ingredients in an instant pot
2. Ace blender and blend until smooth.

Nutrition:

- Calories: 295
- Protein: 18 grams
- Total Fat: 5 grams
- Carbohydrates: 44 grams

ORANGE, CARROT & KALE SMOOTHIE

Preparation Time: 5 mins

Cooking Time: 0 mins

Servings: 1

Ingredients:

- 1 carrot, peeled
- 1 orange, peeled
- 1 stick of celery
- 1 apple, cored 2oz kale
- ½ teaspoon matcha powder

Directions:

1. Place all of the ingredients into a blender and add in enough water to cover them.
2. Process until smooth, serve and enjoy.

Nutrition:

- Calories: 156 Cal
- Fat: 1 g
- Fiber: 7 g
- Carbs: 68 g
- Protein: 5 g

PEANUT BUTTER CUP PROTEIN SHAKE

Preparation Time: 5 mins

Cooking Time: 0 mins

Servings: 2

Ingredients:

- 1 banana, peeled
- 1 scoop of chocolate protein powder
- 1 tablespoon nutritional yeast
- tablespoons peanut butter
- ½ cup almond milk, unsweetened
- Extra: ½ teaspoon turmeric powder

Directions:

1. Place all the ingredients in the order into a food processor or blender, and then pulse for 1 to 2 minutes until smooth.
2. Distribute smoothie between two glasses and then serve.
3. Meal Prep Instructions: Divide smoothie between two jars or bottles, cover with a lid, and then store the containers in the refrigerator for up to 3 days.

Nutrition:

- Calories: 233 Cal
- Fat: 11.1 g
- Fiber: 0 g
- Carbs: 18.6 g
- Protein: 14.6 g

PEANUT BUTTER AND STRAWBERRY SMOOTHIE

Preparation Time: 5 mins

Cooking Time: 0 mins

Servings: 2

Ingredients:

- ounces strawberry bananas, peeled, sliced
- tablespoons peanut butter
- 1 ½ cup almond milk, unsweetened

Directions:

1. Place all the ingredients in the order into a food processor or blender, and then pulse for 1 to 2 minutes until smooth
2. Distribute smoothie between two glasses and then serve.
3. Meal Prep Instructions: Divide smoothie between two jars or bottles, cover with a lid and then store the containers in the refrigerator for up to 3 days.

Nutrition:

- Calories: 238 Cal
- Fat: 9.8 g
- Fiber: 4.5 g
- Carbs: 32.1 g
- Protein: 5.3 g

PINEAPPLE & CUCUMBER SMOOTHIE

Preparation Time: 5 mins

Cooking Time: 0 mins

Servings: 1

Ingredients:

- 2oz cucumber
- 1 stalk of celery slices of fresh pineapple sprigs of parsley
- ½ teaspoon matcha powder
- Squeeze of lemon juice
- Serves 1 77 calories per serving

Directions:

1. Place all of the ingredients into blender with enough water to cover them and blitz until smooth.

Nutrition:

- Calories: 77 Cal

RASPBERRY VANILLA SMOOTHIE

Preparation Time: 5 minutes

Cooking time: 5 minutes

Servings: over 2 cups

Ingredients:

- 1 cup frozen raspberries
- A 6-ounce container of vanilla Greek yogurt
- ½ cup of unsweetened vanilla almond milk

Directions:

1. Take all your ingredients and place them in an instant pot Ace blender.
2. Process until smooth and liquified.

Nutrition:

- Calories: 155
- Protein: 7 grams
- Total Fat: 2 grams
- Carbohydrates: 30 grams

Preparation Time: 5 mins

Cooking Time: 0 mins

Servings: 1

Ingredients:

- 3oz kale 2oz strawberries
- 1 apple, cored sticks of celery
- 1 tablespoon parsley
- 1 teaspoon of matcha powder
- Squeeze lemon juice (optional) to taste

Directions:

1. Place the ingredients into a blender and add enough water to cover the ingredients and blitz to a smooth consistency.

Nutrition:

- Calories: 101 Cal
- Fat: 1 g
- Fiber: 1 g
- Carbs: 12 g
- Protein: 10 g

SOURSOP SMOOTHIE

Preparation Time: 5 minutes

Cooking Time: 5 Minutes

Servings: 2

Ingredients:

- 3 quartered frozen Burro Bananas
- 1-1/2 cups of Homemade Coconut Milk
- 1/4 cup of Walnuts
- 1 teaspoon of Sea Moss Gel
- 1 teaspoon of Ground Ginger
- 1 teaspoon of Soursop Leaf Powder
- 1 handful of kale

Directions:

1. Prepare and put all ingredients in a blender or a food processor.
2. Blend it well until you reach a smooth consistency.
3. Serve and enjoy.

Nutrition:

- Calories: 213
- Fat: 3.1g
- Carbs: 6g
- Protein: 8g

SPINACH AND BERRY SMOOTHIE

Total time: 10 minutes

Preparation time: 10 minutes
Cooking time: 0 minutes
Servings: 2

Ingredients:
- 1 cup blackberries
- 1 avocado, pitted, peeled and chopped
- 1 banana, peeled and roughly chopped
- 1 cup baby spinach
- 1 tablespoon hemp seeds
- 1 cup water
- ½ cup almond milk, unsweetened

Directions:
1. In your blender, mix the berries with the avocado, banana, spinach, hemp seeds, water and almond milk.
2. Pulse well, divide into 2 glasses and serve for breakfast.
3. Enjoy!

Nutrition:
- Calories 160,
- Fat 3,
- Fiber 4,
- Carbs 6,
- Protein 3

STRAWBERRY RHUBARB SMOOTHIE

Preparation Time: 8 minutes

Cooking time: 0 minute

Servings: 1

Ingredients:

- 1 cup strawberries, fresh & sliced
- 1 rhubarb stalk, chopped
- 2 tablespoons honey, raw
- 3 ice cubes
- 1/8 teaspoon ground cinnamon
- ½ cup Greek yogurt, plain

Directions:

1. Start by getting out a small saucepan and fill it with water.
2. Place it over high heat to bring it to a boil, and then add in your rhubarb.
3. Boil for three minutes before draining and transferring it to a blender.
4. In your blender add in your yogurt, honey, cinnamon, and strawberries.
5. Blend until smooth, and then add in your ice.
6. Blend until there are no lumps and it's thick. Serve cold.

Nutrition:

- 201 Calories
- 11g Fats
- 39g Protein

SWEET CRANBERRY NECTAR

Preparation Time: 8 minutes

Cooking time: 5 minutes

Servings: 4

Ingredients:

- 4 cups fresh cranberries
- 1 fresh lemon juice
- ½ cup agave nectar
- 1 piece of cinnamon stick
- 1-gallon water, filtered

Directions:

1. Add cranberries, ½ gallon water, and cinnamon into your pot
2. Close the lid Cook on HIGH pressure for 8 minutes
3. Release the pressure naturally
4. Firstly, strain the liquid, then add the remaining water
5. Cool, add agave nectar and lemon
6. Served chill and enjoy!

Nutrition: (Per Serving)

- Calories: 184
- Fat: 0g
- Carbohydrates: 49g
- Protein: 1g

VEGAN BLUEBERRY SMOOTHIE

Preparation Time: 5 minutes

Cooking Time: 0 minutes

Servings: 2

Ingredients:
- 2 cups blueberries
- 1 tbsp hemp seeds
- 1 tbsp chia seeds
- 1 tbsp flax meal
- 1/8 tsp orange zest, grated
- 1 cup fresh orange juice
- 1 cup unsweetened coconut milk

Directions:
1. Toss all your ingredients into your blender, then process till smooth and creamy.
2. Serve immediately and enjoy.

Nutrition:
- Calories: 212
- Fat: 6.6g
- Carbs: 36.9g
- Protein: 5.2g

WALNUT & DATE SMOOTHIE

Preparation Time: 10 minutes

Cooking time: 0 minute

Servings: 2

Ingredients:

- 4 dates, pitted
- ½ cup milk
- 2 cups Greek yogurt, plain
- 1/2 cup walnuts
- ½ teaspoon cinnamon, ground
- ½ teaspoon vanilla extract, pure
- 2-3 ice cubes

Directions:

1. Blend everything until smooth, and then serve chilled.

Nutrition:

- 109 Calories
- 11g Fats
- 29g Protein

BLACKBERRY CHEESECAKE KETO BREAKFAST SMOOTHIE

Preparation time: 5 minutes

Servings: 1

Ingredients:

- ½ cup frozen blackberries
- ¼ cup (2 oz) cream cheese
- sweetener of your choice, to taste
- 1 Tbsp coconut oil or MCT oil
- ¼ tsp vanilla extract
- pinch of salt
- ¼ cup coconut milk
- ½ cup water

Directions:

1. Add all ingredients to a blender and blend until smooth.
2. Serve and enjoy!

Nutrition:

- Calories: 459
- Sugar: 10g
- Fat: 41g
- Carbs: 14g
- Fiber: 4g
- Protein: 5g

CHOCOLATE PEANUT BUTTER KETO SMOOTHIE

Preparation time: 5 min

Servings: 1

Ingredients:

- ¼ cup creamy peanut butter
- 3 Tbsp cocoa powder
- 1½ cup unsweetened almond milk
- 1 cup heavy cream or coconut cream
- 6 Tbsp powdered erythritol (to taste)
- A pinch of sea salt (optional)

Directions:

1. Combine all ingredients in a blender.
2. Puree until smooth.
3. Adjust sweetener as desired.

Nutrition:

- Calories: 435
- Fat: 41g
- Protein: 9g
- Net Carbs: 6g
- Fiber: 4g
- Sugar: 3g

Preparation time: 2 minutes

Servings: 1

Ingredients:

- 1 cup milk for the almond.
- 1 scoop Perfect Oil Powder Keto MCT
- 1 Vanilla Whey Protein Powder Perfect Keto scoop.
- 2 ice cubes
- ½ tsp cinnamon

Directions:

1. Blend all ingredients until smooth.
2. Serve immediately.

Nutrition:

- Calories: 223
- Fat 11.5g
- Carbs 4g
- Fiber 3.7g
- Protein 25.1g

COCONUT CHERRY VANILLA SMOOTHIE

Preparation time: 1 minute

Servings: 1

Ingredients:

- 2 ½ oz full-fat canned coconut milk
- 3 ½ oz filtered water
- A pinch of pure vanilla powder
- A pinch oFinely ground sea salt
- 3 oz frozen organic cherries
- 7-8 ice cubes

Directions:

1. Blend all the ingredients.
2. Serve immediately.

Nutrition:

- Calories: 216
- Fat: 17g
- Saturated Fat: 15g
- Sodium: 15mg
- Potassium: 375mg
- Carbs: 17g
- Fiber: 3g
- Sugar: 13g

CUCUMBER CELERY MATCHA KETO GREEN SMOOTHIE

Preparation time:5 min

Servings: 1

Ingredients:

- ½ cup cashew milk
- 1 baby cucumber
- 1 stalk celery
- ½ avocado
- 1 Tbsp coconut oil
- 1 tsp matcha powder
- Sweetener of choice, to taste

Directions:

1. Put all ingredients in a blender and mix until smooth.
2. Serve and enjoy!

Nutrition:

- Calories: 278
- Sugar: 2g
- Fat: 27g
- Carbs: 12g
- Fiber: 6g
- Protein: 3g

STRAWBERRY SMOOTHIE

Preparation time: 5 minutes

Servings: 2

Ingredients:

- ¼ cup heavy whipping cream
- ¾ cup unsweetened original almond milk
- 2 tsp granulated stevia/erythritol blend (Pyure)
- 4 oz frozen strawberries
- ½ cup ice
- ½ tsp vanilla extract

Directions:

1. Place all ingredients in blender.
2. Pulse until blended, if necessary, scraping down the sides.
3. Serve in 2 large glasses.

Nutrition:

- Calories: 152
- Fat: 13g
- Carbs: 5g
- Fiber: 1g
- Protein: 1g,
- Net carbs: 4g

STRAWBERRY VANILLA SMOOTHIE

Preparation time: 2 minutes

Servings: 1

Ingredients:

- ½ cup fresh or frozen strawberries
- ⅓ cup unsweetened coconut milk
- 2/3 cup water
- ½ tsp vanilla extract

Directions:

1. Blend all ingredients until smooth.
2. Serve immediately.

Nutrition:

- Calories: 149
- Fat: 11g
- Carbs: 8g
- Fiber: 2g
- Protein: 6g

EGGNOG SMOOTHIE

Prep time: 5 min

Servings: 1

Ingredients:

- ¼ cup heavy whipping cream or coconut cream
- ¼ tsp ground cloves
- ½ tsp cinnamon
- 1 egg
- 1 tsp Erythritol
- 1 tsp Sugar-Free Maple Syrup (optional)

Directions:

1. Blend all ingredients until smooth.
2. Serve immediately.

Nutrition:

- Calories: 320
- Fat: 30g
- Saturated Fat: 17g
- Cholesterol: 186mg
- Carbs: 8g
- Fiber: 2g
- Protein: 6g

PECAN PIE SMOOTHIE

Preparation time: 10 minutes

Serving: 1

Ingredients:

- 3/4 cup almond, hemp, or coconut milk without sweetening.
- 1 SGF Vanilla Creamer spoonful.
- 2 cubic meters of raw or lightly toasted pecans.
- 2 spoonfuls of ground flaxseed.
- 1 Tbsp cashew or butter with macadamia.
- 1 tsp cinnamon from Ceylon.
- Sea salt.

Directions:

1. Add all ingredients until silky smooth in a blender and puree.
2. Chill in the fridge for 15 to 20 min if you want a thicker smoothie, then drink.

Nutrition:

- Fat 36 g
- Protein 7 g
- Fiber 8 g
- Carb: 13 g
- Net Carb: 5 g

STRAWBERRY AVOCADO SMOOTHIE

Preparation time: 2 minutes

Servings: 1

Ingredients:

- 1 lb frozen strawberries
- 1 large avocado
- ¼ cup Erythritol (or another sweetener)
- 1 ½ cup unsweetened almond milk

Directions:

1. Blend all ingredients until smooth.
2. Serve immediately.

Nutrition:

- Calories: 106
- Fat: 7g
- Protein: 1g
- Net Carbs: 7g
- Fiber: 5g
- Sugar: 4g

AVOCADO SMOOTHIE

Preparation Time: 10 Minutes

Cooking Time: 0 Minutes Servings: 2

Ingredients:
- 1 Avocado, ripe & pit removed
- 2 cups Baby Spinach
- 2 cups Water
- 1 cup Baby Kale
- 1 tbsp. Lemon Juice
- 2 sprigs of Mint
- ½ cup Ice Cubes

Directions:
1. Place all the ingredients needed to make the smoothie in a high-speed blender and blend until smooth.
2. Transfer to a serving glass and enjoy it.
3. Tip: If you want to add more sweetness, you can add a pinch of honey.

Nutrition:
- Calories: 214
- Carbohydrates: 15g
- Proteins: 2g
- Fat: 17g
- Sodium: 25mg

AVOCADO TURMERIC SMOOTHIE

Preparation Time: 5 Minutes

Cooking Time: 2 Minutes

Servings: 1

Ingredients:

- ½ of 1 Avocado
- 1 cup Ice, crushed
- ¾ cup Coconut Milk, full-fat
- 1 tsp. Lemon Juice
- ¼ cup Almond Milk
- ½ tsp. Turmeric
- 1 tsp. Ginger, freshly grated

Directions:

1. Place all the ingredients excluding the crushed ice in a high-speed blender and blend for 2 to 3 minutes or until smooth.
2. Transfer to a serving glass and enjoy it.
3. Tip: If desired, you can add a pinch of pepper to it.

Nutrition:

- Calories: 232
- Carbohydrates: 4.1g
- Proteins: 1.7g
- Fat: 22.4g
- Sodium: 25mg

BANANA & STRAWBERRY SMOOTHIE

Preparation Time: 7 minutes

Cooking Time: 0 minute

Serving: 2

Ingredients:
- 1 banana, sliced
- 4 cups fresh strawberries, sliced
- 1 cup ice cubes
- 6 oz. yogurt
- 1 kiwi fruit, sliced

Directions:
1. Add banana, strawberries, ice cubes and yogurt in a blender.
2. Blend until smooth.
3. Garnish with kiwi fruit slices and serve.

Nutrition:
- Calories: 54
- Carbohydrate: 11.8g
- Protein: 1.7g

BERRY MINT SMOOTHIE

Preparation Time: 5 Minutes
Cooking Time: 5 Minutes
Servings: 2

Ingredients:

- 1 tbsp. Low-carb Sweetener of your choice
- 1 cup Kefir or Low Fat-Yoghurt
- 2 tbsp. Mint
- ¼ cup Orange
- 1 cup Mixed Berries

Directions:

1. Place all the ingredients needed to make the smoothie in a high-speed blender and blend until smooth.
2. Transfer the smoothie to a serving glass and enjoy it.
3. Tip: You can add flax seeds or chia seeds if you prefer to make it more nutritious.

Nutrition:

- Calories: 137
- Carbohydrates: 11g
- Proteins: 6g
- Fat: 1g
- Sodium: 64mg

BERRY & SPINACH SMOOTHIE

Preparation Time: 11 minutes

Cooking Time: 0 minute

Serving: 2

Ingredients:

- 2 cups strawberries
- 1 cup raspberries
- 1 cup blueberries
- 1 cup fresh baby spinach leaves
- 1 cup pomegranate juice
- 3 tablespoons milk powder (unsweetened)

Directions:

1. Mix all the ingredients in a blender.
2. Blend until smooth.
3. Chill before serving.

Nutrition:

- Calories: 118
- Carbohydrate: 25.7g
- Protein: 4.6g

BLACKBERRY SMOOTHIE

Preparation Time: 5 Minutes

Cooking Time: 0 Minutes

Servings: 1

Ingredients:

- 1 ½ cups Almond Milk
- ¼ cup Cauliflower, blanched & frozen
- 1 Orange
- 1 tbsp. Flax Seed
- 1/3 cup Carrot, grated
- 1 tsp. Vanilla Extract

Directions:

1. Place all the ingredients needed to make the blackberry smoothie in a high-speed blender and blend for 2 minutes until you get a smooth mixture.
2. Transfer to a serving glass and enjoy it.
3. Tip: Instead of cauliflower, you can also use blanched & frozen zucchini.

Nutrition:

- Calories: 275
- Carbohydrates: 9g
- Proteins: 11g
- Fat: 17g
- Sodium: 73mg

BLUEBERRY SMOOTHIE

Preparation Time: 5 Minutes

Cooking Time: 2 Minutes

Servings: 2

Ingredients:

- 1 tbsp. Lemon Juice
- 1 ¾ cup Coconut Milk, full-fat
- ½ tsp. Vanilla Extract
- 3 oz. Blueberries, frozen

Directions:

1. Combine coconut milk, blueberries, lemon juice, and vanilla extract in a high-speed blender.
2. Blend for 2 minutes for a smooth and luscious smoothie.
3. Serve and enjoy.
4. Tip: If desired, you can add more lemon juice to it for more tanginess.

Nutrition:

Calories: 417

Carbohydrates: 9g

Proteins: 4g

Fat: 43g

Sodium: 35mg

CANTALOUPE & PAPAYA SMOOTHIE

Preparation Time: 9 minutes

Cooking Time: 0 minute

Serving: 2

Ingredients:

- ¾ cup low-fat milk
- ½ cup papaya, chopped
- ½ cup cantaloupe, chopped
- ½ cup mango, cubed
- 4 ice cubes Lime zest

Directions:

1. Pour milk into a blender.
2. Add the chopped fruits and ice cubes.
3. Blend until smooth.
4. Garnish with lime zest and serve.

Nutrition:

- Calories: 207
- Carbohydrate: 18.4g
- Protein: 7.7g

CINNAMON ROLL SMOOTHIE

Preparation time: 10 minutes

Cooking time: 0 minutes

Servings: 1

Ingredients:

- 1 tsp. Flax Meal or oats, if preferred
- 1 cup Almond Milk
- 1/2 tsp. Cinnamon
- 2 tbsp. Protein Powder
- 1 cup Ice
- ¼ tsp. Vanilla Extract
- 4 tsp. Sweetener of your choice

Directions:

1. Pour the milk into the blender, followed by the protein powder, sweetener, flax meal, cinnamon, vanilla extract, and ice.
2. Blend for 40 seconds or until smooth.
3. Serve and enjoy.

Nutrition:

- Calories: 145
- Carbs: 1.6g
- Proteins: 26.5g
- Fat: 3.25g
- Sodium: 30mg

COCONUT SPINACH SMOOTHIE

Preparation Time: 5 Minutes

Cooking Time: 0 Minutes

Servings: 2

Ingredients:

- 1 ¼ cup Coconut Milk
- 2 Ice Cubes
- 2 tbsp. Chia Seeds
- 1 scoop of Protein Powder, preferably vanilla
- 1 cup Spin

Directions:

1. Pour coconut milk along with spinach, chia seeds, protein powder, and ice cubes in a high-speed blender.
2. Blend for 2 minutes to get a smooth and luscious smoothie.
3. Serve in a glass and enjoy it.
4. Tip: You can avoid protein powder if not desired.

Nutrition:

- Calories: 251
- Carbohydrates: 10.9g
- Proteins: 20.3g
- Fat: 15.1g
- Sodium: 102mg

GREENIE SMOOTHIE

Preparation Time: 5 Minutes

Cooking Time: 5 Minutes

Servings: 2

Ingredients:

- 1 ½ cup Water
- 1 tsp. Stevia
- 1 Green Apple, ripe
- 1 tsp. Stevia
- 1 Green Pear, chopped into chunks
- 1 Lime
- 2 cups Kale, fresh
- ¾ tsp. Cinnamon
- 12 Ice Cubes
- 20 Green Grapes
- ½ cup Mint, fresh

Directions:

1. Pour water, kale, and pear in a high-speed blender and blend them for 2 to 3 minutes until mixed.
2. Stir in all the remaining ingredients into it and blend until it becomes smooth.
3. Transfer the smoothie to serving glass.

Nutrition:

- Calories: 123
- Carbohydrates: 27g
- Proteins: 2g
- Fat: 2g

KEY LIME PIE SMOOTHIE

Preparation Time: 5 Minutes

Cooking Time: 0 Minutes

Servings: 1

Ingredients:

- ½ cup Cottage Cheese
- 1 tbsp. Sweetener of your choice
- ½ cup Water
- ½ cup Spinach
- 1 tbsp. Lime Juice
- 1 cup Ice Cubes

Directions:

1. Spoon in the ingredients to a high-speed blender and blend until silky smooth.
2. Transfer to a serving glass and enjoy it.
3. Tip: Instead of water, you can use almond milk to make it more nutritious and creamier.

Nutrition:

- Calories: 180
- Carbohydrates: 7g
- Proteins: 36g
- Fat: 1g
- Sodium: 35mg

OATS COFFEE SMOOTHIE

Preparation Time: 5 Minutes

Cooking Time: 5 Minutes

Servings: 2

Ingredients:
- 1 cup Oats, uncooked & grounded
- 2 tbsp. Instant Coffee
- 3 cup Milk, skimmed
- 2 Banana, frozen & sliced into chunks
- 2 tbsp. Flax Seeds, grounded

Directions:
1. Place all the ingredients in a high-speed blender and blend for 2 minutes or until smooth and luscious.
2. Serve and enjoy.
3. Tip: If you need more sweetness, one teaspoon of any low-carb sweetener.

Nutrition:
- Calories: 251Kcal
- Carbohydrates: 10.9g
- Proteins: 20.3g
- Fat: 15.1g
- Sodium: 102mg

ORANGE CARROT SMOOTHIE

Preparation Time: 5 Minutes

Cooking Time: 0 Minutes

Servings: 1

Ingredients:

- 1 ½ cups Almond Milk
- ¼ cup Cauliflower, blanched & frozen
- 1 Orange 1 tbsp. Flax Seed
- 1/3 cup Carrot, grated
- 1 tsp. Vanilla Extract

Directions:

1. Mix all the ingredients in a high-speed blender and blend for 2 minutes or until you get the desired consistency.
2. Transfer to a serving glass and enjoy it.

Tip: If you want to make it more nutritious, you can add collagen powder.

Nutrition:

- Calories: 216
- Carbohydrates: 10g
- Proteins: 15g
- Fat: 7g
- Sodium: 25mg

PEANUT BUTTER BANANA SMOOTHIE

Preparation Time: 5 Minutes

Cooking Time: 2 Minutes

Servings: 1

Ingredients:

¼ cup Greek Yoghurt, plain

½ tbsp. Chia Seeds

½ cup Ice Cubes

½ of 1 Banana

½ cup Water

1 tbsp. Peanut Butter

Directions:

1. Place all the ingredients needed to make the smoothie in a high-speed blender and blend to get a smooth and luscious mixture.
2. Transfer the smoothie to a serving glass and enjoy it.
3. Tip: If desired, you can add chocolate chips to it.

Nutrition:

- Calories: 202
- Carbohydrates: 14g
- Proteins: 10g
- Fat: 9g
- Sodium: 30mg

PEANUT BUTTER SMOOTHIE WITH BLUEBERRIES

Preparation Time: 12 minutes

Cooking Time: 0 minute

Serving: 2

Ingredients:

- 2 tablespoons creamy peanut butter
- 1 cup vanilla almond milk (unsweetened)
- 6 oz. soft silken tofu
- ½ cup grape juice
- 1 cup blueberries
- Crushed ice

Directions:

1. Mix all the ingredients in a blender.
2. Process until smooth.

Nutrition:

- Calories: 247
- Carbohydrate: 30g
- Protein: 10.7g

PEACH & APRICOT SMOOTHIE

Preparation Time: 11 minutes

Cooking Time: 0 minute

Serving: 2

Ingredients:

- 1 cup almond milk (unsweetened)
- 1 teaspoon honey
- ½ cup apricots, sliced
- ½ cup peaches, sliced
- ½ cup carrot, chopped
- 1 teaspoon vanilla extract

Directions:

1. Mix milk and honey.
2. Pour into a blender.
3. Add the apricots, peaches and carrots.
4. Stir in the vanilla.
5. Blend until smooth.

Nutrition:

- Calories: 153
- Carbohydrate: 30g
- Protein: 32.6g

RASPBERRY AND PEANUT BUTTER SMOOTHIE

Preparation Time: 10 minutes

Cooking Time: 0 minute

Serving: 2

Ingredients:

- Peanut butter, smooth and natural [2 tbsp]
- Skim milk [2 tbsp]
- Raspberries, fresh [1 or 1 ½ cups]
- Ice cubes [1 cup]
- Stevia [2 tsp]

Directions:

1. Situate all the ingredients in your blender.
2. Set the mixer to puree.
3. Serve.

Nutrition:

- Calories: 170
- Fat: 8.6g
- Carbohydrate: 20g

STRAWBERRY CHEESECAKE SMOOTHIE

Preparation Time: 5 Minutes
Cooking Time: 0 Minutes
Servings: 1

Ingredients:
- ¼ cup Soy Milk, unsweetened
- ½ cup Cottage Cheese, low-fat
- ½ tsp. Vanilla Extract
- 2 oz. Cream Cheese
- 1 cup Ice Cubes
- ½ cup Strawberries
- 4 tbsp. Low-carb Sweetener of your choice

Directions:
1. Add all the ingredients for making the strawberry cheesecake smoothie to a high-speed blender until you get the desired smooth consistency.
2. Serve and enjoy.
3. Tip: Instead of soy milk, you can also use almond milk or water.

Nutrition:
- Calories: 347
- Carbohydrates: 10.05g
- Proteins: 17.5g
- Fat: 24g
- Sodium: 45mg

STRAWBERRY, KALE AND GINGER SMOOTHIE

Preparation Time: 13 minutes

Cooking Time: 0 minute

Serving: 2

Ingredients:

- Curly kale leaves, fresh and large with stems removed [6 pcs]
- Grated ginger, raw and peeled [2 tsp]
- Water, cold [½ cup]
- Lime juice [3 tbsp]
- Honey [2 tsp]
- Strawberries, fresh and trimmed [1 or 1 ½ cups]
- Ice cubes [1 cup]

Directions:

1. Position all the ingredients in your blender.
2. Set to puree. Serve.

Nutrition:

- Calories: 205
- 2.9g Fat

TROPICAL SMOOTHIE

Preparation Time: 8 minutes

Cooking Time: 0 minute

Serving: 2

Ingredients:

- 1 banana, sliced
- 1 cup mango, sliced
- 1 cup pineapple, sliced
- 1 cup peaches, sliced
- 6 oz. nonfat coconut yogurt
- Pineapple wedges

Directions:

1. Freeze the fruit slices for 1 hour.
2. Transfer to a blender.
3. Stir in the rest of the ingredients except pineapple wedges.
4. Process until smooth.
5. Garnish with pineapple wedges.

Nutrition:

- Calories: 102
- Carbohydrate: 22.6g
- Protein: 2.5g

WATERMELON & CANTALOUPE SMOOTHIE

Preparation Time: 10 minutes

Cooking Time: 0 minute

Serving: 2

Ingredients:

- 2 cups watermelon, sliced
- 1 cup cantaloupe, sliced
- ½ cup nonfat yogurt
- ¼ cup orange juice

Directions:

1. Add all the ingredients to a blender.
2. Blend until creamy and smooth.
3. Chill before serving.

Nutrition:

- Calories: 114
- Carbohydrate: 13g
- Protein: 4.8g

AVOCADO & SPINACH SMOOTHIE

Preparation time: 10 minutes

Serves: 2

Ingredients:

- 2 C. fresh baby spinach
- 1 tbsp. hemp seeds
- 3-4 drops liquid stevia
- ½ of avocado, peeled, pitted and chopped
- ½ tsp. ground cinnamon
- 2 C. chilled filtered water

Directions:

1. In a high-speed blender, add all ingredients and pulse until smooth.
2. Transfer into 2 serving glasses and serve immediately.

Nutrition:

- Calories: 132
- Fat: 11.7g
- Carbs: 6.1g
- Fiber: 4.5g
- Sugar: 0.4g
- Protein: 3.1g
- Sodium: 27mg

BERRY SMOOTHIE

Preparation time: 5 min

Cooking time: 0 min

Servings: 2

Ingredients:

- 1 cup blackberries
- 1 cup strawberries
- 1 cup blueberries
- 1 cup low-fat yogurt

Directions:

1. Put all ingredients in the blender and blend until you get a smooth mixture.
2. Pour the cooked smoothie in the glasses.

Nutrition:

- Calories: 183
- Protein: 9g
- Carbs: 31.6g
- Fat: 2.3g
- Fiber: 7g
- Cholesterol: 7mg
- Sodium: 88mg
- Potassium: 569mg

CHOCOLATY AVOCADO SMOOTHIE

Preparation time: 10 minutes

Cooking time: 8 minutes

Serves: 2

Ingredients:

- 1 medium avocado, peeled, pitted and chopped
- ½ tsp. organic vanilla extract
- ¼ C. ice cubes
- 1 small banana, peeled and sliced
- 3 tbsp. cacao powder
- 1¾ C. chilled fat-free milk

Directions:

1. In a high-speed blender, add all ingredients and pulse until smooth.
2. Transfer into 2 serving glasses and serve immediately.

Nutrition:

- Calories: 358
- Fat: 21.3g
- Carbs: 36.5g
- Fiber: 10g
- Sugar: 18.4g
- Protein: 11g
- Sodium: 121mg

CUCUMBER & GREENS SMOOTHIE

Preparation time: 10 minutes

Serves: 2

Ingredients:

- 1 small cucumber, peeled and chopped
- ½ C. lettuce, torn
- ¼ C. fresh mint leaves
- 1 tsp. fresh lemon juice
- ¼ C. ice cubes
- 2 C. mixed fresh greens
- ¼ C. fresh parsley leaves
- 2-3 drops liquid stevia
- 1½ C. filtered water

Directions:

1. In a high-speed blender, add all ingredients and pulse until smooth.
2. Transfer into 2 serving glasses and serve immediately.

Nutrition:

- Calories: 50
- Fat: 0.5g
- Carbs: 11.3g
- Fiber: 3.6g
- Sugar: 3.2g
- Protein: 2.5g
- Sodium: 34mg

KIWI & CUCUMBER SMOOTHIE

Preparation time: 10 minutes

Serves: 2

Ingredients:

- 2 kiwis, peeled and chopped
- 2 tbsp. fresh cilantro leaves
- 2-3 drops liquid stevia
- 1 medium cucumber, peeled and chopped
- ½ tsp. fresh ginger, peeled and chopped
- 2 C. filtered water

Directions:

1. In a high-speed blender, add all ingredients and pulse until smooth.
2. Transfer into 2 serving glasses and serve immediately.

Nutrition:

- Calories: 71
- Fat: 0.6g
- Carbs: 17g
- Fiber: 3.1g
- Sugar: 9.4g
- Protein: 1.9g
- Sodium: 6mg

GRAPES & KALE SMOOTHIE

Preparation time: 10 minutes

Serves: 2

Ingredients:

- 2 C. fresh kale, trimmed and chopped
- 3-4 drops liquid stevia
- 1½ C. filtered water
- 1 C. seedless green grapes
- 1 tbsp. fresh lime juice
- ¼ C. ice cubes

Directions:

1. In a high-speed blender, add all ingredients and pulse until smooth.
2. Transfer into 2 serving glasses and serve immediately.

Nutrition:

- Calories: 65
- Fat: 0.2g
- Carbs: 15g
- Fiber: 1.4g
- Sugar: 7.5g
- Protein: 2.3g
- Sodium: 30mg

GREEN VEGGIE SMOOTHIE

Preparation time: 10 minutes

Serves: 2

Ingredients:
- 1 C. fresh spinach
- ½ of small green bell pepper, seeded and chopped
- 2 C. chilled filtered water
- ¼ C. broccoli florets, chopped
- ¼ C. green cabbage, chopped
- 3-4 drops liquid stevia

Directions:
1. In a high-speed blender, add all ingredients and pulse until smooth.
2. Transfer into 2 serving glasses and serve immediately.

Nutrition:
- Calories: 132
- Fat: 11.7g
- Carbs: 6.1g
- Fiber: 4.5g
- Sugar: 0g
- Protein: 0.4g
- Sodium: 18mg

GREEN PROTEIN DETOX SMOOTHIE

Prep Time: 3 Mins

Total Time: 3 Mins

Ingredients

- ½ cup unsweetened almond milk
- 1 tablespoon almond butter
- 1 banana
- 2 cups baby spinach

Directions:

1. Wash all the detox smoothie ingredients.
2. Add weight loss smoothie ingredients to the blender starting with the greens and ending with the fruit.
3. Blend until smooth, adding more water until you reach your desired green detox smoothie consistency.

Nutrition:

- Calories: 237
- Fat: 11.4g
- Saturated Fat: 1g
- Fiber: 6.5
- Protein: 6.9g
- Carbohydrates: 33.1

MANGO PINEAPPLE GREEN SMOOTHIE

Preparation Time: 3 minutes

Servings: 2

Ingredients:

- 1 cup frozen mango chunks
- 1 cup frozen pineapple chunks
- 1 cup fresh spinach or kale
- 1¼ cups orange juice
- ½ cup nonfat plain or vanilla Greek yogurt
- 1 tablespoon ground flaxseed
- 1 teaspoon granulated stevia

Directions:

1. Situate all of the ingredients in the pitcher of a blender.
2. Purée until smooth.
3. Serve immediately

Nutrition:

- Calories: 213
- Total Fat: 2g
- Sodium: 44mg
- Potassium: 582mg
- Total Carbohydrate: 43g
- Protein: 9 g

ORANGE AND PINEAPPLE GREEN SMOOTHIE

Prep Time: 5 Mins

Total Time: 5 Mins

Ingredients

- 2 baby spinach, handfuls
- 2 naval oranges, small (peeled and seeded)
- Frozen pineapple chunks (slightly less than a ⅓ of a 16oz bag)
- Light coconut milk

Directions:

1. Place baby spinach and coconut milk into the blender and blend for a few seconds to break up the spinach.
2. Add in the oranges and frozen pineapple, then blend until completely smooth.
3. Enjoy!

Nutrition:

- Fat: 5.5g
- Carbohydrates: 23.3g
- Sugar: 16.9g
- Sodium: 26.8mg
- Fiber: 3.7g
- Protein: 1.7g

CONCLUSION

One of the difficulties most kidney patients encounter is seeking simple, delicious recipes for CKD that help them control the amounts in their blood of chemicals and fluid.

This book tries to reach a healthy ground between savoring your food's flavor and having the dietary change necessary.

The goal of this diet is to maintain the electrolyte, mineral, and fluid levels in your body healthy while you are on dialysis with CKD.

15942615R00064